The Essential tı
Rhine river cruise: Glossary of interesting places and attractive tourism locations every tourist should know and explore

Rigel Pollux

COPYRIGHT

Table of Contents

Introduction

Emma was a young woman who formerly resided in a little village tucked away on the banks of the Rhine River. Her heart yearned to discover the magnificent vistas and quaint villages that the Rhine had to offer, and she had always fantasized about setting out on a great adventure.

Emma saw a strange sight as she was gazing out at the glistening waves one beautiful morning. A gorgeous river cruise vessel in royal blue and sparkling white floated elegantly into view. It appeared as though fate had come to her door. Emma gathered her stuff without thinking twice and headed towards the ship.

She entered the ship and was immediately enthralled by its beauty and allure. The crew showed her to her comfortable stateroom, which had a balcony with views of the Rhine, and gave her a warm welcome. Emma was ready to go out on the trip of a lifetime, and she couldn't control her enthusiasm.

With the help of the calm Rhine currents, the ship set sail. Emma discovered herself surrounded by strangers from all over the world, each with their own experiences and goals. Bonds were forged as they exchanged jokes, tales, and cultural experiences that went beyond language and boundaries.

As the ship chugged through the magnificent scenery of Switzerland, France, Germany, and the Netherlands, days went into weeks. Emma was in awe of the medieval castles towering above hills, their storied histories rustling in the breeze. She visited quaint villages known for their cobblestone walkways, bustling marketplaces, and friendly residents.

Emma learned about each location's rich history and cultural assets on guided tours. She admired the majesty of the Cologne Cathedral, explored the cobblestone streets of Strasbourg's old town, and became lost in the creative splendor of Amsterdam's world-famous institutions.

Emma's heart, however, was really stolen in the interim. Emma found comfort on the sun-kissed deck, surrounded by stunning vistas of vineyards, rolling hills, and lovely villages, as the ship sailed through the gorgeous Rhine Gorge. Her own spirit of exploration was reflected in the river's soft rhythm.

The night was a magical moment. Emma had

delicious meals cooked by skilled chefs, enjoyed vivacious music and entertainment, and danced under the stars with new acquaintances. The ship transformed into a mobile oasis of joy where there was constant companionship and laughter.

Emma's heart was overflowing with appreciation as the Rhine River cruise came to an end for the incredible experience she had. She had learned about the Rhine River's charm, the beauty of connection, and the strength of adventure. She would cherish the experiences she experienced for the rest of her life as a reminder of the transformational impact of pursuing one's aspirations.

And so Emma carried the spirit of adventure inside her as she said goodbye to the ship and the new acquaintances who had become her family. After her Rhine River trip, she felt inspired and eager to see the globe. She knew that the Rhine had kindled a flame that would eternally direct her on her own unique path.

A Rhine River cruise is a captivating voyage that takes you into the heart of Europe and enables you to learn about the region's natural beauty, historical significance, and cultural riches. One of the most famous and significant rivers on the continent, the Rhine flows from the Swiss Alps to the North Sea for around 1,230 kilometers (760 miles).

Leaving on a Rhine River cruise gives you a fresh perspective as you pass beautiful scenery, quaint villages, and historical sites. You will pass through several nations on the tour, including Switzerland, France, Germany, and the Netherlands, giving you the chance to explore the various cultures, architectural styles, and cuisines of each place.

There are many fascinating sites to take in as you travel down the Rhine. Every stop along the road has a fascinating narrative to tell, from medieval villages with their winding alleyways and half-timbered buildings to fairytale-like castles situated on hilltops and old Roman ruins. A UNESCO World Heritage site, the Rhine Gorge is well known for its breathtaking cliffs, vineyards, and the fabled Loreley Rock.

More than simply historical sights and visual splendor may be found on a Rhine River cruise. You'll get the chance to travel to exciting cities like Cologne, Strasbourg, and Amsterdam, each of which offers a unique combination of historic and contemporary sights, cultural activities, and delectable cuisine. The Rhine River cruise offers an engaging and fascinating experience, whether you want to visit renowned museums, wander through attractive ancient villages, or indulge in regional wines and specialties.

You will sail in luxury and grandeur the entire time aboard a river cruise ship furnished with contemporary conveniences and opulent quarters. You can choose to unwind on the deck while taking in the expansive views of the passing scenery or take part in one of the onboard activities or shows. You will be taken on immersive tours of important places by professional guides who will share insights into the history, art, and culture of the area.

An effortless way to discover a variety of locations along this renowned waterway, a Rhine River cruise is a great option for both novice and experienced visitors. A Rhine River cruise ensures a fascinating and enlightening experience, regardless of your interests in history, art, nature, or just absorbing the allure of Europe.

Chapter One

What every tourist need to know about Rhine river cruise

- Season and Itinerary: Rhine River cruises offer a range of itineraries, from quick excursions to more extensive journeys. Find the cruise itineraries that best fit your interests and time constraints by researching several cruise alternatives. Also take into account the season, as spring and summer provide nice temperatures and bright sceneries, while fall delivers gorgeous foliage and celebrations of the wine harvest

- Popular Ports: Stops at well-known ports including Cologne, Strasbourg, Basel, and Amsterdam are frequently included on Rhine

River cruises. To make the most of your stay in each location, schedule your shore excursions in advance since these ports offer a plethora of historical, cultural, and architectural treasures.

- Excursions and Activities: A variety of guided shore excursions are frequently offered on river cruises, and they are typically included in the cruise fare. These tours provide you the chance to see the city's top sights and discover its history and culture. For a more immersive experience, think about adding extras like wine tastings, bike excursions, or trips to the neighborhood markets.

- Scenic Highlights: The beautiful Rhine Gorge, filled with castles and vineyards, is one of the Rhine River's most striking natural features. Don't pass up the chance to unwind on the ship's deck while cruising down the river and taking in the expansive sights. To capture the beauty of the surroundings and the quaint villages you pass by, keep your camera close at hand.

- Cultural Immersion: The Rhine region is rich in history and culture; thus, spend some time becoming involved in the customs of the area. To get a better understanding of the locations you visit, sample local foods and wines, go to cultural events, and engage with the welcoming residents.

- Onboard facilities: To further your comfort and enjoyment, river cruise ships provide a variety of facilities. These could include roomy accommodations with private balconies, great onboard dining options, relaxing bars and lounges, and even health amenities like spas and fitness centers. To maximize your time onboard, become familiar with the ship's facilities.

- Wears: Casual wear is often accepted on river cruises, which normally have a liberal dress code. Packing a couple somewhat more formal clothing is a smart idea because certain ships may feature dressier evenings. For detailed dress code requirements, check with the cruise line.

- Packing Essentials: Include items like sturdy walking shoes, layered, lightweight clothes that can be thrown on and taken off as the weather changes, a hat and sunglasses for sun protection, a waterproof jacket, and a power adaptor if necessary. Don't forget to pack any required travel paperwork, prescription drugs, and information on travel insurance.

- Money & Payments: Depending on whatever nation you are in, several currencies are utilized in the Rhine area. For modest transactions or situations where credit cards might not be accepted, it is recommended to have some local cash on hand. Although a lot of establishments in well-known tourist locations do take credit cards, it's always a good idea to have some cash with you.

- River Cruise Etiquette: Follow correct etiquette to show respect for the ship's personnel and other guests. Be careful of noise levels, observe designated smoking areas, and, if necessary, observe mealtimes and clothing standards. To guarantee a good experience for everyone, keep in mind to be on time for excursions.

By following these suggestions, you'll be well-equipped for a memorable and pleasurable Rhine River cruise, enabling you to fully experience the area's alluring beauty and cultural diversity.

Important Rhine River Cruise Tips for Tourists

- Plan Ahead and do your investigate: Before setting off on a Rhine River cruise, thoroughly investigate the various cruise companies, itineraries, and ports of call. To select the trip that best meets your demands, take into account your tastes, hobbies, and spending capacity. To make the most of your time in each location, schedule your shore excursions and other activities in advance.

- Pack Wisely: Bring lightweight, adaptable clothing that can be worn in a variety of climates. For shore excursions, you must wear shoes that are comfortable to stroll in. Bring a compact day bag to take your necessities on excursions, and don't forget your reusable water bottle, sunscreen, and hat.

- Be Ready for Various Currencies: The Rhine River flows through several nations, each of which has its own currency. Have some local money on hand for smaller purchases, and a credit card on hand for bigger ones. To prevent any card problems, it's also a good idea to let your bank know about your vacation intentions.

- Drink plenty of water and use sunscreen: The sun may be very strong while on a summer cruise. Stay hydrated by drinking lots of water, and shield your eyes from the sun's rays by using sunglasses, a hat, and sunscreen.

- Take Advantage of Onboard facilities: For your comfort and enjoyment, river cruise ships provide a variety of facilities. Utilize the amenities onboard, including as the clubs, gyms, and spa services. Take part in the entertainment and activities offered aboard to make the most of your voyage.

- Participate in Local Culture: Get involved in the community by tasting out local food, going to cultural events, and mingling with the populace. Learn a few simple words and expressions in the native tongue to express your respect and gratitude.

- Be Punctual: To guarantee a seamless experience for everyone, be on time for shore excursions and activities. Inaccuracies in the ship's timetable might affect the entire journey.

- Respect Local Customs and the Environment: As you travel down the Rhine, keep in mind the regional traditions and the environment. Observe any special instructions given by the cruise personnel, and respect regional traditions. Respect the neighborhood and properly dispose of rubbish.

- Stay Connected and Informed: Keep up with events, meal times, and any itinerary changes by checking the ship's daily schedule, announcements, and updates. Access critical information or maintain contact with loved ones by using the onboard Wi-Fi or other communication methods.

- Unwind and Enjoy: Keep in mind that a Rhine River cruise is a holiday, so give yourself some time to unwind and take in the scenery. Enjoy the wonderful food, take in the breathtaking landscape, and create lifelong memories with your fellow travelers. Allow yourself to relax and take in the river's beauty and peace.

You'll be ready for a seamless, fun, and memorable Rhine River cruise journey if you bear these crucial suggestions in mind.

Chapter Two

Glossary of interesting Rhine river cruise interesting locations

Alsatian Wine Route (FR): Take a gorgeous trip through picturesque vineyards, quaint villages, and rolling hills along the Alsatian Wine Route. Enjoy wine tastings, tour family-owned wineries, and discover the local winemaking customs.

Amsterdam (NL): Even though Amsterdam is not on the Rhine, many Rhine river excursions terminate or start there. Discover the city's well-known canals, see world-renowned institutions like the Rijksmuseum and Van Gogh Museum, and take in the energetic vibe.

Andernach (DE): Visit the Roman fort, "the largest Roman military installation north of the Alps," to learn more about Andernach's remarkable Roman past. Visit the ancient Town Hall, take a leisurely stroll along the Rhine promenade, and be sure to see the renowned "Round Tower," a 56-meter-tall defense structure.

Andernach Food Market (DE): Enjoy the great meals at the Andernach meals Market, where neighborhood sellers sell a variety of fresh vegetables, regional delicacies, and mouthwatering street food. Enjoy traditional cuisine while soaking in the lively ambiance of this bustling market.

Andernach Geysir (DE): At Andernach, see the

tallest cold-water geyser in the world. Visit the Namedyer Werth peninsula by boat to see the stunning water eruptions, which may reach heights of up to 60 meters.

Antwerp (BE): another gem of Belgium, is well-known for its booming diamond and fashion sectors. Explore the city's historic district, take in some mouthwatering Belgian chocolates, and visit the magnificent Antwerp Cathedral.

Arnhem (NL): Visit the renowned John Frost Bridge and the Airborne Museum, which are both known for their World War II heritage. Visit the Kröller-Müller Museum, which has a remarkable art collection, and explore the Hoge Veluwe National Park, which is home to a variety of flora and animals.

Assmannshausen (DE): Visit the picturesque Assmannshausen hamlet, known for its red wines and picturesque location. Visit nearby vineyards, take a leisurely stroll along the Rhine promenade, and take in the tranquil ambiance.

Bacharach (DE): A gorgeous riverfront location and a quaint medieval village with well-preserved half-timbered homes. Visit Stahleck Castle, stroll around the town walls, and try regional wines in a quaint pub.

Bacharach Wine Village (DE): Visit the quaint wine hamlet of Bacharach, which is well-known for its vineyards and winemaking. Take a visit of a nearby vineyard, sip some of the mouthwatering Rieslings produced there, and take in the medieval ambience as you meander through the little lanes.

Basel (CH): A bustling metropolis famed for its museums and arts scene. Enjoy the Rhine promenade, the Kunstmuseum Basel, and a stroll around the old town.

Basel Paper Mill Museum (CH): Explore the Basel Paper Mill Museum to learn more about the evolution of papermaking. Discover the fully operational paper mill from the fifteenth century, discover conventional papermaking methods, and attempt to make your own paper.

Bernkastel-Kues (DE): This charming village is well known for its vineyards and half-timbered homes that have been maintained. Explore the medieval marketplace, taste some regional wines, and take in the expansive vistas of the Moselle River.

Bingen am Rhein: which is situated at the entrance to the Upper Middle Rhine Valley, is a combination of historical significance and scenic beauty. Take a tour of the Burg Klopp stronghold, cruise the Rhine, and hike or cycle through the nearby vineyards.

Bonn (DE): Ludwig van Beethoven was born in Bonn, which is a thriving cultural center with a number of museums, including the Beethoven House. Take a stroll along the Old Town's lovely Old Rhine promenade.

Boppard (DE): take in the splendor of the Rhine Gorge. Explore the historic town center, take a chairlift trip to the Vierseenblick viewpoint for panoramic views, and unwind by the river promenade.

Boppard Roman Fort (DE): The Upper Germanic-Rhaetian Limes, a UNESCO World Heritage Site, including the Roman Fort of Boppard. Discover the fortification's well-preserved ruins, discover Roman military life, and take in the picturesque Rhine Valley vistas.

Bruges (BE): Although Bruges is not located immediately on the Rhine, Antwerp may take a side excursion there. Its well-preserved medieval buildings, flowing canals, and romantic ambiance have made this city a UNESCO World Heritage Site.

Cochem (DE): A charming village tucked away in the Moselle Valley that is well-known for its romantic Reichsburg Castle. Take a lovely trek or bike ride along the river, stroll through the quaint alleyways dotted with half-timbered buildings, and try some local wine.

Cologne Cathedral (Cologne, DE): A beautiful Gothic cathedral renowned for its exquisite stained glass windows and remarkable construction.

Drachenburg Castle (DE): Go to the fanciful Drachenburg Castle, which is located close to Königswinter and positioned high on a hill overlooking the Rhine. Admire the castle's architecture, stroll around the lovely gardens, and take in the expansive views of the river and surrounding area.

Duisburg (DE): take in the industrial history of the Rhine area. Explore the Innenhafen, a bustling collection of restaurants and museums, and the Landschaftspark Duisburg-Nord, a former ironworks turned cultural and recreational park.

Düsseldorf (DE): Well-known for its cutting-edge construction, exciting nightlife, and upscale shopping. Discover the hip Medienhafen neighborhood, take in the panoramic views at the Rheinturm, and stroll through the opulent Königsallee.

Eberbach Abbey (DE): Explore the magnificent Eberbach Abbey, a former Cistercian abbey from the 12th century. Discover the ancient cloister, the stunning architecture of the abbey, and it's fascinating history by taking a guided tour.

Eglisau (CH): Explore the Rhine River's banks to find the historic village of Eglisau. Explore the lovely promenade, take in the restored half-timbered homes, and savor the tranquil atmosphere of this dreamy Swiss town.

Eltville (DE): a charming town well-known for its vineyards and wineries, is situated in the center of the Rheingau wine region. Explore the lovely rose garden, tour the Electoral Castle, and partake in wine tastings at nearby estates.

Ghent (BE): a charming city worth seeing even if it is not immediately on the Rhine if your cruise takes you farther into BE. Explore the historic buildings, go to St. Bavo's Cathedral to see the renowned Ghent Altarpiece, and wander along the quaint canals.

Heidelberg Castle (DE): A grand ruined castle that once towered above Heidelberg and was renowned for its romantic ambiance and lovely gardens.

Kinderdijk (NL): This is a UNESCO World Heritage Site known for its 19 recognizable windmills. Take a historical tour of water management, a trip to the museum mill, and a picturesque bike or boat tour of the region.

Koblenz (DE): Visit the Electoral Palace, a spectacular mansion displaying Rococo and Classicist architecture, while exploring Koblenz's ancient old town. Enjoy the lively ambiance of the city while taking a leisurely stroll around the Schloss Bellevue's grounds.

Koblenz Cable Car (DE): For stunning views of

the Rhine and Moselle rivers, ride the Koblenz Cable Car, popularly referred to as the Seilbahn Koblenz. The cable car provides a distinctive view of the city and the surroundings as it travels between the Ehrenbreitstein Fortress and the Deutsches Eck.

Koblenz Electoral Palace (DE): Tour Koblenz's majestic Electoral Palace, a remarkable illustration of French Classicism in design. Visit the rich interiors, including the sumptuous state rooms and the lovely grounds, on a guided tour.

Lahnstein (DE): Visit the charming village of Lahnstein, which is situated where the Rhine and Lahn rivers meet. Visit Lahneck Castle, take a leisurely stroll along the Rhine promenade, and take in the tranquil beauty of the surroundings.

Linz am Rhein (DE): renowned for its restored medieval architecture, is a lovely town well worth seeing. Explore the winding alleys, see the old town hall, and take in the lovely half-timbered homes.

Lorelei Rock (DE): A mythological Rhine cliff with breathtaking vistas and connections to mythology. Through history, many poems and songs have been inspired by it.

Loreley Visitor Center (DE): you may learn about the myths and tales associated with the Loreley Rock. Enjoy interactive displays that bring the legends to life as you learn about the tales, myths, and songs that are linked with this famous cliff.

Luxemborg City (LU): Discover the spectacular Casemates du Bock, stroll down the Chemin de la Corniche, and take in this attractive city's diverse atmosphere.

Mainz (DE): A city with a fascinating ancient town and a long history. Explore the magnificent Mainz Cathedral while learning about printing's history at the Gutenberg Museum.

Mainz Gutenberg Museum (DE): Spend some time at the Mainz Gutenberg Museum getting lost in the history of printing. Explore historic manuscripts, visit Gutenberg's first printing press, and study the social effects of the printing revolution.

Mannheim (DE): The origin of the Mannheim School of classical music, a city with a long history in music. Discover the Baroque Mannheim Palace, have a peaceful escape in the Luisenpark, and attend a concert at the Mannheim National Theatre.

Marksburg Castle (DE): The lone hilltop castle on the Rhine that has escaped destruction, providing sweeping views of the river and the region.

Nierstein (DE): which is well-known for its wine-making, is a charming village tucked away among vineyards. Visit a local winery with a guide, sample some of the well regarded Rieslings, and take in the breathtaking scenery of the surrounding area.

Nijmegen (NL): Take a tour of the oldest city in Netherland, which has a long Roman history. Discover the city's thriving cultural and gastronomic scene by visiting the Valkhof Museum and taking a stroll along the Waal River.

Obernai (FR): a historic town in the heart of the Alsace region. Visit the majestic St. Peter and St. Paul Church and stroll the cobblestone streets while admiring the vibrant half-timbered homes.

Oberwesel (DE): Take through Oberwesel's impressively preserved medieval towers and walls.

Explore the Schönburg Castle, stroll around the town walls, and discover the Loreley Rock's lore.

Reichenstein Castle (DE): Visit the charming Castle, which is perched on a hilltop above the Rhine. Enjoy the breathtaking views of the river valley and the castle's intriguing history by taking a guided tour.

Remagen (DE): Discover the tranquil village of Remagen and stop at the famous Ludendorff Bridge, which was crucial in the Second World War. Discover the history of the Peace Museum and the events that took place there.

Rhine Falls (Schaffhausen, CH): The biggest waterfall in Europe, with spectacular vistas and an exhilarating experience. To come up close to the falls, take a boat trip.

Rotterdam (NL): discover the cutting-edge and contemporary side of the Netherlands. Admire the distinctive architecture, go shopping in Markthal, and enjoy a boat trip of Europe's biggest harbor.

Rüdesheim (DE): A quaint community well-known for its wineries and vineyards. Don't overlook the Drosselgasse, a little street lined with wine bars and venues for live music.

Saarburg (DE): a picturesque town perched on a hillside next to the Saar River. Explore the quaint ancient neighborhood, take a boat excursion down the river, and admire the lovely waterfall in the middle of the city.

Speyer (DE): Is the location of the magnificent Speyer Cathedral, a UNESCO World Heritage site renowned for its spectacular architecture and housing the biggest Romanesque crypt on earth. For a wonderful collection of historic automobiles, airplanes, and more, go to the Technik Museum Speyer.

St. Goar (DE): a charming town famous for Burg Rheinfels, a fortified castle from the Middle Ages. Take a leisurely stroll along the riverbank, see the castle remains, and enjoy the expansive views of the Rhine.

St. Goarshausen (DE): Visit the picturesque village of St. Goarshausen, which is the location of the renowned Loreley Rock. Discover the regional stories and folklore while seeing the Rheinfels Castle and taking in the picturesque views from the riverbank promenade.

Strasbourg (FR): A charming city with a fusion of German and French characteristics. Take a boat excursion around the canals, see the city's historic core, and see the magnificent Strasbourg Cathedral.

Trier (DE): which is regarded as DE's oldest city, is a veritable gold mine of Roman history. Explore the ruins of the Imperial Baths, have a look at the historic Roman Bridge, and stop at the Porta Nigra, the biggest Roman city gate north of the Alps.

Wiesbaden (DE): Here is a posh spa town famed for its opulent architecture and warm spas. Visit the Kurhaus, take a leisurely stroll down the magnificent Wilhelmstrasse, and unwind in one of the luxury baths.

Worms (DE): Explore the spectacular Worms Cathedral, one of DE's greatest specimens of Romanesque architecture, which is renowned for its historical significance. Learn about the city's contribution to the Protestant Reformation as you tour one of Europe's oldest Jewish cemeteries.

Xanten (DE): an archaeological site that displays the ruins of a Roman city, to travel back in time. Explore the Roman Museum, visit the rebuilt amphitheater, and get a taste of life in ancient Rome.

Xanten Archaeological Park (DE): allows visitors to see Roman history come to life. Explore the rebuilt Roman city, the amphitheater, the hot baths, and the Roman homes to gain an understanding of daily life in the past.

Zaanse Schans (NL): Visit this outdoor museum to travel back in time, which has wooden cottages, workshops, and authentic Dutch windmills. Discover the area's industrial history, observe artisans at work, and take in the beautiful surroundings.

Zons (DE): Explore the well-preserved city walls and towers of Zons, a medieval walled town. Visit the Zonser Grindsmühle, stroll through the quaint alleyways surrounded with half-timbered homes, and take in the serene ambiance.

Printed in Great Britain
by Amazon